The Fractured Shards

Jennifer Dellow

Copyright © 2015 Jennifer Dellow

All rights reserved.

ISBN-13: 978-1511555975

ISBN-10:1511555971

DEDICATION

To my Rose, my Keystone, my Mirror and my Honeybee
Always.

CONTENTS

Acknowledgments i

Apology Part One – Dear Heart
I'm flying away because I'm lonely
The snake has coiled
It seems the air does blind us
Smile alone or with the memory
The Lady
Apology Part Two – Dear Mind
Starring up the grass does shimmer
Every Breath
We stand here now in pieces
The Wind
A cooling calm that covers
They say death is like flying
Sharp black spindles
Apology Part Three – Dear Soul
Like a cat I have nine lives
Have you seen the stranger?
I live in a jar
I write letters to a man
My Dear, my darling companion
Looking through black trees
There is a knife
You can die from being sad
The sky is calling
The Snowglobe
Step through into a mirror
I have stared out of this window
Falling

ACKNOWLEDGMENTS

To all those poets before me who gave me inspiration and nurtured the love of words.

Apology Part One – Dear Heart

As if you didn't have enough;
with each thump through my chest.
I really hoped you wasn't right,
but you always knew best

Blood-stained and in a thousand pieces;
I did nothing but watch you shatter.
Wishing there was something more to say,
but knowing no words will ever matter.

Each beat is becoming lighter;
and the rhythm is shallow.
It's not whole and there's a space-
that'll always lie fallow.

The blood that I have lost-
can never be replaced.
When I now look in the mirror;
every day I will be faced.

I let my heart be taken outwards.
It's now as heavy as a tome.
In fear and lost amongst the darkness-
will it find a way home?

Jennifer Dellow

I'm Flying Away Because I'm Lonely

I'm flying away because I'm lonely.
Maybe I'll feel at one with the air.
Existing but not seen by anybody.
It can choke and give life with no care.

I'm lonely because nobody sees me.
A thing that is easily done.
The turmoil it creates in my being.
A yearning to turn my face to the sun.

I'm invisible because of the noises.
The perpetual dripping of a tap.
There is a bridge that connects rational thinking.
I have the bridges – each complete with a gap.

I'm listening because I'm a thinker.
It's solid which nothing can change.
I'm hopeful this flight brings new beginnings.
Once the door is unhooked from my cage.

The Snake Has Coiled

The snake has coiled; its soothing roughness;
Like the rope which ensnares a boat
Its weaved its way up the spine of my soul
To slither and link around my throat

It had been telling me that it was coming
I thought I could heal and make it tame
Each word it says is a poisoned arrow
Shutting my heart – my face aflame

The stock of its poison has become lowered
The fight began at the tolling bell
It wants me to fire some venom backwards
But I see its eyes – I don't want it in hell

The hiss and the noise is a constant comfort
Like new parents and their baby's breath
The pain and elation as it smothers all feeling
Like seeking great happiness at planning your death

I am my worst enemy – I gave it a home here
I have given a burglar the key to my door
Take it up or over – some powers still with me
He's with me at sunrise or if I kneel on the floor

Jennifer Dellow

It seems the air does blind us

It seems the air does blind us
I am trapped by what I see
The reflection in a teardrop
Does nothing to comfort me

The loudness of an echo
The past bouncing off the walls
Some longing to touch the face;
Reply once more to its calls

Pain that never stops growing
Darkness has clouded the eyes
I want to rewind the music
And wish we'd not severed those ties

Smile Alone Or With The Memory

Smile alone or with the memory
Existing when you snap your fingers
Trying to wash away the turmoil
But the scent still lingers

A face that's full of torment
Silent eyes that bring a chill
Try and cut away dead flesh
But the scar won't heal

Heightened words and expectation
Causes need to have a fix
The ripple forever spreading
But the clock still ticks

Jennifer Dellow

The Lady

The lady glides amongst the silver
It's not a dress – she's bathed in light
She only appears amongst the winter
Spending seasons out of sight

She holds your pale and frozen fingers
When you seek the silky moon
When you fear – you want her guidance
She comforts you; and tells you "soon"

The lady has no voice or features
And yet you hear and see her well
Just like the hearts rhythmic beating
Reassuring – a tolling bell

My eyes look up – I search my future
Whilst mixing this past and present place
There is a mirror that gives no reflection;
Just liquid life flowing from my face

The lady stands and points a finger
Here and now – in amongst the blue
Across the lake she's found my mirror
The fractured shard of a different hue

Apology Part Two – Dear Mind

I was such a private person
There should only ever be
A locked gate to you my darling
But I'm afraid I lent the key

I let somebody hold it
Because I thought that I held theirs
I didn't, and they made copies
Which were tossed away with no cares

All the beads of thinking
Like bubbles blown away.
Every word that passed the threshold
And every word about to say

In an act of self-protection
A second gate has now been chained
My love for you kept on growing
Your love for me quickly waned

The actions out of kindness
Stirred an echo that was violent
A part of me has left the room
That will remain forever silent

Jennifer Dellow

Staring Up The Grass Does Shimmer

Staring up the grass does shimmer
You're the one who won't let me be
The world doesn't turn – complete the circle
Until you turn your face to me

Moving up to see the sun down
It's always there and made of white
I've lost my name – myself and ego
No more thoughts or desire to fight

Every Breath

Every breath draws air into the chasm
It's a toxin I cannot repel
It gives life as it diseases the body
Everyone walks when they're born but I fell

I shook hands with myself many years back
The eyes reflected a joy from the pain
I had met the other half of my spirit
No rejoice; but my feelings wont wane

It's too much to expect things will change now
I am fragile – all I want is to run
What if it fades because it's fake and I'm lonely?
Like a painting left for years in the sun

The world revolves it's a circular motion
I'm only allowed to follow the path of the square
Early/late; out of sync/step; all timings
Placed on life's journey without paying the fare

I hope that someday all is forgiven
I tried and did the best that I could
Let the dust of peace settle upon me
And let my face be revealed from the hood

Jennifer Dellow

We Stand Here Now In Pieces

We stand here now in pieces
There's no-one left to calm the sea
The worst of the worst; but it's not over
We still fall – but look to me

You hit me hardest when I saw you
That look – I'll never be the same
Follow to heaven, hell or limbo
Take your weakness, fear and shame

Looking upwards the sky is starless
We are blind to others dreams
Let's create our new beginning
Stand together, we are seams

The Wind

The wind howls through
My mind – at last feels clear.
With each blow from the sky,
It carried my dreams.

I saw the moon;
Clean amongst the dark.
A brightness which filled my
Eyes; as if it were you.

Clouds don't know time,
They stretch across lands;
With the poise of a cat.
Delicate – yet firm.

I will edge towards Fortune;
But my heart wills me to run.
Every time that I see him,
I know I've come home.

Jennifer Dellow

A Cooling Calm That Covers

A cooling calm that covers
I wear it like I'm proud
It comes and goes as if its winter
Across my face just like a shroud

People fear the darkness
For me it's a second home
Counting days until eternal slumber
The years I've had are out on loan

They Say Death Is Like Flying

They say death is like flying;
I can vouch, say it's true
But death is less feared than being in love
Especially when in love with you

They say death is like sleeping
It can control all you do
But my world has stopped turning
Because the world turns with you

They say life is worth living
I can vouch, say it's true
Because my life is now brighter
Since the day I loved you

Sharp Black Spindles

Sharp black spindles
Blot the grey sky
She's the only one who thinks
He only questions why

They want to give us names
Because it makes them feel good
Put the scarf around your neck
Hide your face in your hood

Half-and-half they fit together
Splintered like the earth and sky
She doesn't need to think things over
He doesn't care the reasons why

Apology Part Three – Dear Soul

I am sorry that I let you
Be dragged through all the wars
Your now ripped and torn edges
As I pulled you from the jaws

Once so over-flowing
Has now become a hole
The light has gone; run out of feeling
Eye windows are now dull

You did send out a warning
A booming signal of alert
Every time they cut my feelings
Every word that's harsh and curt

It's not that I ignored it
I just hoped I wasn't wrong
As they took away my music,
Words; my thoughts – my only song

I wish I could repair it
But I've run out of the thread
A life which could have had a purpose
A life – a part of which is dead

Jennifer Dellow

Like A Cat I Have Nine Lives

Like a cat I have nine lives
I've already mislaid four
One was brain – and then potion
One was heart and then the door

I do not trust my heart
It gives me painful pleasure
Because it lacks sense of the brain
So it can never properly measure

Have You Seen The Stranger?

Have you seen the stranger;
Who creeps around at night?
He wants to live in darkness
Whilst taking all your light.

He appears in many guises
A friend, a lover or a clown.
He despises when you're happy
Only satisfied if you're down.

His soul is completely empty
But weighs heavy, like a tome.
He preys on all your fears
And makes your mind his home.

I Live In A Jar

I live in a jar
It's a constant vacuum
Do I want to break out
Or let it become my tomb?

The world and its noise
They drown out my cries
They see me without looking
Their stare magnifies

But someone can hear me
Although they deny what they feel
He can control all my feelings
With the turn of a wheel

The fear is now spreading
When was love ever a rash?
But he's there holding a hammer –
And I want him to smash

I Write Letters To A Man

I write letters to a man
Who never writes to me
Every moment spent with him
Allows me to be free

Some nights I feel alone
So I look and find my star
It gives me comfort knowing it's there
No matter how afar

I'm sorry that I cried last night
Although it's best to let me be
If you want there to be an us
You must accept all parts of me

I tried to talk to you again
But I struggled with what to say
Every time I fail to tell you
I feel like I've lost a day

Every time I let you in
I feel happy, content and free
You fail to realize all the time
That you're the first to see

I've written letters to a man
Who doesn't write back at all
And yet he's my star – a pillar of hope
The one who won't allow me to fall?

Jennifer Dellow

My Dear, My Darling Companion

My dear, my darling companion
With hope that this letter sends
That you'll remember the better times together
Which caused us to be such good friends

I know that things weren't always easy
Our minds turning just like the seas
We'd locked out so many people
And hidden away all of the keys

Think of the times we almost created new beginnings
Instead of the times that we just about coped
You as a friend was never regretful
It was everything; just as I'd hoped

Like trees in a storm that was brewing
We didn't break; but we were forced to bend
The wind's gone but the days keep on flowing
Maybe time could be the scaffold that'll mend

I wish that it could have been different
I cannot tell you how much I have tried
We've been changed of what we should be
A part of me will forever be quiet

The reason I liked you was simply
The soul in your body was you
No malicious bone or intention
A simple look and we both just knew

And yet maybe I've been in a bubble
There's a fog; an un-lifted haze
I looked at you and saw something special
Conjuring hope for the rest of my days

Looking Through Black Trees

Looking through black trees
Where the sun once glimmer
Red amongst the blue
Tepid water can simmer

Honey meets the sand
It's strange how they mix
They each bring calmness
But no agenda or tricks

A life amongst the breeze
Is my world overdue
I've paid enough soul
I want my kindness in lieu

There Is A Knife

There is a knife
Which carves the wood
No mistakes are made
It does what it should

The heart is heavy;
The mind is free
The knife has no feelings
As it jabs at me

The books was closed
The blade opened it up
The pages are flowing
Like tea from a cup

The words softly spoken
Has opened a vein
I'm at the steps of a castle
I've become the new Jane

You Can Die From Being Sad

You can die from being sad
It's a terrible disease
It can make your mind shut down
It can bring you to your knees

It's a slow and painful death
Each person's cure is unique
As it cripples how you're breathing
And your heart will slowly leak

It's like standing on a pier
And wanting to jump in
Or gathering up a cord
And committing ultimate sin

Have you ever wished that
You'd simply said nothing at all?
To suffer how things were
Must be better than hearing Him call

It's the constant weight of pain
That will get you in the end
It can be lifted by one person
Who has the ability to mend

So you wait for their arrival
As it gets harder with every breath
Wishing that they would come quickly
Because the alternative is death

You can die from being sad
I am at that place right now
But I don't think he is going to save me
I can feel my heart…..fail

The Sky is calling

The sky is calling,
people push past.
My heart is sinking,
I'm fading fast.

The man is coming;
but he holds no fear.
I've met him already,
at the start of the year.

I'll find him when ready
and it's not going to be soon.
There's someone to talk to,
I want to look at the moon.

I own every moment;
each day will be mine.
Regardless of sunset,
the date or the time.

The carriage is nearing.
The man thinks he will win.
But there's somebody near me,
and I think we're akin.

The Snowglobe

My life is a snow globe.
A delicate orb;
a vacuum of intensity.

The slightest brush throws
all my thoughts asunder.
And I am left - to wait.

For the water to calm me
as I gaze stoic, at each speck,
which falls.

Jennifer Dellow

Step through into the mirror

Step through into the mirror;
there you'll find a different life.
Liquid future - Solid Present,
each little shard is like a knife.

Pull it out and pull it open,
you will always have your words.
Filling your head just like the ocean;
or flying high amongst the birds.

Limbs are weaker; eyes are dizzy;
and your body is shutting down.
But your mind won't crumble - it's not ready,
you can never flee this town.

Expect the worst and mull things over;
we only fear when we are winning.
You could turn it off and stop the dance,
but the record will keep on spinning.

The Fractured Shards

I have stared out of this window

I have stared out of this window
with feelings I could no longer quell.
I knew I would never be happy;
and all I could hear was the bell.

I'd searched every inch of my future,
longing for a comfortable space.
I knew I should never be happy;
your eyes refused to look at my face.

The Sun provokes nothing but sadness.
For I can cloak my tears with the rain.
I knew I could never be happy;
back on the edge once again.

His eyes lured me into the cliff face.
Different body; but the soul is the same.
Oh Lord, how I long to be happy;
and meet the spirit who can relight the flame.

Falling

Falling deep in to
a darker state of mind
I'm slipping; and yet
someone brings me the gift
of light
and sees me
for who I am

ABOUT THE AUTHOR

Jennifer Dellow is a 30 year old life aficionado with a desire to allow all parts of her personality to have the floor. She has had a passion for poetry and prose since her childhood which has continued vehemently into her adulthood.

Another of Jennifer's poetry collections is currently published through Channillo.com which is a serialized literature subscription site.

Jennifer lives in England and when she's not writing, she enjoys obsessing over David Bowie and Orson Welles. You can follow her on Twitter or visit her blog https://ninjanerdflewlone.wordpress.com for more delirious insights into her world.

Twitter: @JenJenJen1385

Book Two of this series is due for release in November 2015.

Printed in Poland
by Amazon Fulfillment
Poland Sp. z o.o., Wrocław